Name

Address

Blank Classic

Composition Notebook
(*Octagonal Pattern*)
97 numbered pages - 100 total pages
Large 8.5 x 11

Blank Classic

Mailing address:
Blank Classic
PO BOX 4608
Main Station Terminal
349 West Georgia Street
Vancouver, BC
Canada, V6B 4A1

Cover design by: Lauren Dick
Interior design by: Lauren Dick

ISBN: 978-1-77476-133-5

FIRST EDITION / FIRST PRINTING

www.ingramcontent.com/pod-product-compliance
Lightning Source LLC
Chambersburg PA
CBHW080306030726
47593CB00009B/2654

* 9 7 8 1 7 7 4 7 6 1 3 3 5 *